THE HOLOCAUST

THE NAZIS SEIZE POWER
1933-1941

Stuart A. Kallen

Published by Abdo & Daughters, 4940 Viking Drive, Suite 622, Edina, Minnesota 55435.

Library bound edition distributed by Rockbottom Books, Pentagon Tower, P.O. Box 36036, Minneapolis, Minnesota 55435.

Printed in the United States.

Cover Photo credit: Bettmann
Interior Photo credits: Wide World photos, pages 6, 19, 22, 29, 32, 35
                     Bettmann, pages 7, 10, 11, 12, 16, 17, 21, 23, 25, 27, 33
                     Archive photos, pages 10, 14, 20, 24

Edited By Rosemary Wallner

Library of Congress Cataloging-in-Publication Data

Kallen, Stuart A., 1955-
    The Nazis Seize Power, 1933-1941 / by Stuart A. Kallen.
        p.   cm. -- (The Holocaust)
    Includes Bibliography and Index.
    ISBN 1-56239-351-0
    1. Holocaust, Jewish (1939-1945) -- Germany--Juvenile literature.
    2. Antisemitism--Germany--Juvenile literature. 3. Germany
    --Politics and government--1933-1945--Juvenile literature.
    I. Title. II. Series: Holocaust (Edina, Minn.)
    DS135.G3315K35   1994
    940.53'18'0943--dc20   94-20144
                                        CIP
                                        AC

TABLE OF CONTENTS

Foreword

The Holocaust is a tragic time in world history. It was a time of prejudice and bias turned to hate and the persecution of an ethnic group by persons who came into a position of power, allowing them to carry out that hate.

The Holocaust series depicts what prejudice and biases can lead to; how men, women and children—simply because they were Jewish—died horrible deaths.

When a child is born it has no prejudices. Bias must be learned and someone has to display it.

The goal of this series is to enlighten children and help them recognize the ignorance of prejudice so that future generations will be tolerant, understanding, compassionate, and free of prejudice.

Acknowledgments:

Rabbi Morris Allen
        Beth Jacob Congregation

Dr. Stewart Ross
        Mankato State University

Special Thanks to The United States Holocaust Memorial Museum

CHAPTER ONE

WITNESSES TO THE FINAL SOLUTION

On April 11, 1945, U. S. Army troops pushed into central Germany. World War II had been raging for more than five years. The conflict had pitted the Axis Powers—Nazi Germany, Italy, Japan, and others—against the Allies—the United States, Great Britain, the Soviet Union, and other countries. Tens of millions of people had been killed in the conflict. Much of Europe was in ruins.

The American soldiers marched into a place called Buchenwald that day. These war-hardened veterans had seen almost every form of horror that one human could visit on another during war. But nothing prepared the soldiers for the sight of the Buchenwald death camp.

Ten thousand dead bodies were stacked in piles like firewood. People who were still alive were human skeletons clothed in rags. Some adults weighed no more than forty pounds. Bugs, disease, and horrid filth were everywhere.

Brick buildings housed gas chambers where tens of thousands of men, women, and children had been gassed by poison shooting out of shower heads. Brick ovens contained bones and ashes from cremated bodies. Boots, suitcases, eyeglasses—even human hair and gold teeth—were stacked in huge piles.

What the Americans had discovered that day was the climax of an official government policy. The government was Nazi Germany and its leader was Adolf Hitler. The policy was "The Final Solution to the Jewish Problem." Hitler and the Nazis had started the official war against Jews 12 years earlier, in the 1933.

American soldiers view with horror a pile of emaciated bodies left in Buchenwald prison camp after the German guards had retreated.

In those twelve years of Hitler's rule, the Nazis had killed six million Jewish people in extermination camps—two-thirds of all the Jews alive in Europe. The Nazis wiped out 2,000 years of European Jewish history. Most of the killing was done in four short years, from 1941 to 1945. The Nazis also killed Gypsies, Jehovah's Witnesses, homosexuals, the mentally ill, and thousands of others who disagreed with them. But, as one survivor of the nightmare, writer Elie Wiesel, said; "Not all victims were Jewish, but all Jews were victims."

This event became known as the Holocaust.

What the troops saw that day in Buchenwald showed what can happen when a government is run by men who are crazy with hatred. Hitler acted with the help of many others. This is the story of how a man, an ideology, and a country began a killing spree that changed the course of world history.

CHAPTER TWO

TWO THOUSAND YEARS OF HATRED

*B*y the end of World War I, Jews had lived in Europe for more than two thousand years. Jews were found in every European country from Portugal to Greece, from Ireland to the Soviet Union. Jews lived in Italy, France, Germany, Bulgaria, Hungary, and especially Poland. These Jewish people trace their beliefs back more than 4,000 years. The Old Testament of the Bible is their Holy Book.

Although the Jews lived in Europe for two millennia, their existence was marred by an almost constant hatred from others, called anti-Semitism. This hatred went back to Biblical times when Christianity was born.

Christianity was bent on replacing Judaism by making the Christian message universal. Early church fathers taught that the only purpose for Jews in history was to prepare for the arrival of Jesus. Jews were expected to leave the scene. Their continued survival seemed an act of stubborn defiance. By the fifth century, anti-Semitism was official church policy. By the Middle Ages, Jews were described by the church as the killers of the Lord Jesus and as the Devil. Stirred up by church liturgy, mobs went on rampages, storming into Jewish towns to rape, murder, and plunder.

By the nineteenth century, the church had relaxed its grip on European society. Jews, while still living on the edges of society, had become doctors, professors, writers, publishers, and other professionals. But many Jews, especially in Eastern Europe, still lived in small towns under primitive conditions not much different than in the Middle Ages.

As the lives of Jews changed, so did the anti-Semitism. Instead of being blamed for the death of God, Jews were blamed for being "racially inferior." This meant that by blood and genetics, Jews could never be as great a race as the white, Christian Europeans.

Richard Wagner, a famous German composer, wrote; "I hold the Jewish race to be the born enemy of pure humanity and everything noble in it. I am perhaps the last German who knows how to hold himself upright in the face of Judaism which already rules everything."

By the beginning of the twentieth century, barriers against Jews were finally beginning to fall. Sigmund Freud, a Jewish thinker, founded the study of psychology. Jewish physicist Albert Einstein launched a new era in science. French Jew Marc Chagall was at the forefront of modern art. And these men were not alone. Between 1905 and 1931 fourteen German Jews were awarded Nobel Prizes in various scientific fields.

In spite of these advances, most Jews were working poor. They were factory workers, carpenters, shopkeepers, and shoemakers. In Eastern Europe, Jews lived in villages, called shtels, that were composed of all Jewish people. They spoke their own language— Yiddish—read Yiddish books, attended Yiddish movies and Yiddish theaters. Most simply strived against the odds to create a happy home for their loved ones.

*Sigmund Freud,
one of the fathers of
psychology.*

*German-born Albert
Einstein (1879-1955),
awarded the Nobel Prize
for Physics in 1922.*

CHAPTER THREE

THE CORNERSTONE
OF NAZISM

*A*nti-Semitism was nothing new in Germany. In fact the term "anti-Semitism" was invented by a German author, Wilhem Marr, in 1873. Marr started the idea of Jews as a separate race, the Semitics. This was a turning point. Before Marr, Jews were considered dangerous because of their religion—what they believed. They could change their beliefs, convert to Christianity, and be considered better. But if they were a race, they simply could not change. This was the cornerstone of Nazi anti-Semitism.

In 1881, an "Anti-Semites Petition" was sent to the leader of Germany. It demanded that Jews be removed from all levels of government. Anti-Semitic politicians were elected to the Reichstag, Germany's ruling body. One of them gave a speech to wild applause that said, "Jews are indeed beasts of prey....The Jews operate like parasites....The Jews are cholera germs." Anti-Semitism was called "the greatest national progress this century."

Anti-Semitic pamphlets and newspapers sprang up throughout all of Nazi Germany.

By 1900, anti-Jewish books and pamphlets appeared everywhere. Some claimed that all good civilization came from blond-haired, blue-eyed, Northern European people, called Aryans. The leaders of this "master race" were Germans. The Aryans said that everything bad came from the Jews.

In 1903, a pamphlet called *The Protocols of the Elders of Zion* was printed in Russia. It was a myth-filled fantasy that said Jews drank children's blood during the Passover holiday. It said that an "international Jewish conspiracy" was taking over the world. By 1920, *The Protocols* had been distributed throughout Europe. In Germany, 120,000 copies had been sold—a huge amount for the time.

"The Eternal Jew," an exhibition of Anti-Semitism in Berlin Germany, 1938.

The Protocols. In 1921, it was proved a forgery—lies from start to finish—but it remained popular. To this very day, people the world over still read and believe the twisted lies printed in *The Protocols.*

CHAPTER FOUR

HITLER AND THE NAZI PARTY

*A*dolf Hitler was born on April 20, 1889, in Austria. As a young man, Adolf Hitler tried his hand as an artist, enrolling in art school in Vienna. He was rejected by the school, so he made his living painting postcards and dwelled in dirty, cheap rooming houses.

Hitler moved to Germany in 1913. He served in the German army in World War I and was wounded twice. After Germany lost the war, Hitler returned to his country to find it in tatters.

Unemployment in Germany was extremely high. There was a bloody revolution in the streets. The Germans had been made to pay for the damage they created in World War I. This made German money worthless. It took a wheelbarrow full of bank notes to buy a loaf of bread. One American penny was worth 1.66 million German marks. The government stood silent while bitter, hungry, angry people tried to fix a blame for their problems. Dozens of new political parties emerged to take advantage of the chaos. Many of these parties were extremely devoted to Germany, super-patriotic, and anti-Semitic.

Adolf Hitler made it to the rank of corporal in the German Army during World War I. Germany was defeated and Hitler was wounded twice.

Thousands of young German men had nothing to do, no work, and no future. The seeds were sown for a violent change.

Hitler joined a small group called the German Workers Party. Eventually, they became the National Socialist German Workers' Party, or the Nazis.

Hitler had a knack for public speaking. He mesmerized crowds. His fiery speeches attracted people to the Nazi Party. The Nazis promised jobs, food, education, and power. They blamed the loss of World War I on the Jews. They put out a program that read, in part:

"Only a racial comrade can be a citizen. Only a person of German blood can be a racial comrade. No Jew, therefore, can be a racial comrade."

But the Jews had fought side by side with the Germans in the German Army in World War I. In fact 100,000 Jews—nearly one-sixth of the Jewish population—had fought in the German Army. Eighty percent of the Jews had combat roles. Thirty-five thousand were decorated for their bravery and twelve thousand lost their lives. Hitler and the anti-Semites ignored these facts.

In 1923, when the German mark became totally worthless, the Nazis tried to take over the government. They failed, and Hitler was arrested. Given a five-year sentence, he spent only eight months in jail. During that time he wrote a book that would become the bible of the Nazi movement. The book was titled *Mein Kampf,* which means "My Struggle" in German. It is the story of Hitler's early life, his political beliefs, and the growth of the Nazi Party.

Mein Kampf is a poorly written book. Most people found it impossible to read. Maybe that is why no one bothered to read what it said at the time. In *Mein Kampf,* Hitler clearly states the Nazi plans for Germany and the Jews. His ideas for the Holocaust are clearly spelled out. Jews are mentioned again and again in *Mein Kampf.* He calls Jews "maggots, vampires, snakes, vermin, plague, and parasites." He says that the Jews are everyone's enemy and he wants to exterminate every last one. *Mein Kampf* states:

> Jews disguise their true purpose by pretending to be a religion, which is the first and greatest lie. They were always a people with definite racial qualities, never a religion.

Finally, Hitler wrote, "World War One might not have been lost if some twelve or fifteen thousand Hebrew corrupters of the people had been poisoned by gas before or during the war."

CHAPTER FIVE

ALL YOU NEED IS HATE

Hatred, burning hatred—that is what we want to pour into the souls of our millions of fellow Germans until the flame of rage ignites our Germany and avenges the corrupters of our nation. — Adolf Hitler

*T*he Nazi Party grew in size. Hitler was a master speaker who controlled the crowds like they were puppets. The masses

laughed, cried, stood on their chairs and shouted when provoked by the wild waving of Hitler's arms. His voice, sounding like a madman shouting at the top of his lungs, hypnotized the audiences.

Hitler dressed up his ravings with the symbols of power. He used an ancient cross called the swastika as his party's symbol. He dressed his followers in black leather boots and brown shirts. He called them storm troopers. He splashed the swastika on a red flag and flew it everywhere.

Hitler used words to promote hatred. The swastika was the official symbol of Nazi Germany.

People yelled "Heil, Hitler" with outstretched arms. Hitler urged his people to go to war—with France, Russia, the United States, Wall Street, and the Jews.

After Nazi rallies, hundreds of storm troopers would burst out of meeting halls looking for Jews to beat up. Sometimes thirty or forty storm troopers would beat one person.

By 1932 the Nazi party was the second largest political party in Germany. In 1933 Hitler was appointed chancellor—prime minister—of Germany. A year later, the German cabinet combined the offices of president and chancellor and made Hitler the supreme and unlimited master of Germany. They called him *der Führer,* the leader. The new government was called the Third Reich.

Hitler reviews 120,000 storm troopers during the Nazi Party Congress at Nuremburg in 1938. Hitler gives the Nazi salute.

CHAPTER SIX

BUILDING THE CAMPS

*T*he first thing Hitler did after seizing power was to abolish Germany's constitution. The Nazis passed an Emergency Decree, "For The Protection Of The People And The State." The decree suspended the right of free speech, free press, the right to assemble, and the privacy of the mails. It also abolished every political party except the Nazi party.

Next Hitler passed the Enabling Act called, "The Law For Terminating The Suffering Of People And Nation." Under the guise of returning Germany from sickness to health, the enabling act allowed the government absolute power to do whatever it pleased. This law allowed the Nazis to search homes and arrest anyone they wanted to for any reason. The first concentration camp, Dachau, was set up to hold these people. The next camp built was Buchenwald. Within a year, fifty concentration camps were built across Germany.

Around him, Hitler assembled a group of men to blindly carry out his orders. Heinrich Himmler ran the Gestapo—the dreaded secret police. They murdered Hitler's enemies including seventy-seven Nazis who Hitler didn't trust. They spied on, arrested, and tortured people. Hitler's second in command, Hermann Goering, was a drug addict, beloved by the Germans for his vicious sense of humor and enjoyment of drink.

Joseph Goebbels was the Nazi "Minister of Public Enlightenment." He held a Ph.D. in literature and philosophy from the University of Heidelberg. Goebbels was in charge of the press.

Hermann Goering was Hitler's second in command. He also headed Germany's airforce, the Luftwaffe.

Joseph Goebbels was the Minister of Public Enlightenment. He was in charge of spreading Nazi propaganda throughout the country.

He controlled all media—newspapers, magazines, radios, movies, theaters, and the arts. Goebbels spread vicious anti-Semitism using the media. He censored every word that the German's heard. Newspapers were licensed and those that did not follow the party line were shut down. Twice a day, Goebbel's ministry held a press briefing to tell reporters how events should be covered. Failure to follow Goebbels's orders resulted in a one-way trip to a concentration camp.

Goebbels said, "If you repeat a lie often enough, people will start to believe it."

Goebbels turned the state-owned broadcasting system into a Nazi propaganda machine. He was one of the first people to realize the power of radio and use it to shape public opinion. Radios were given away to the public so that Goebbels could spread the Nazi message. Goebbels had a great speaking voice and he was the most popular Nazi speaker after Hitler.

The Schutzstaffel or SS was the black-shirted security squad of elite Nazis. It was headed by Heinrich Himmler. Doctors, professors, lawyers, and other professionals were chosen for their devotion to Hitler. Their symbol of the SS was a skull and crossbones.

Heinrich Himmler, head of the Schutzstaffel or the SS.

The Schutzstaffel or SS was the most feared group in the Nazi regime. Their symbol was the skull and crossbones and their job was simply to terrorize.

The SS conducted door-to-door searches looking for Hitler's enemies. They rounded up Jews, Communists, Socialists, clergymen, trade union members, people who listened to foreign radio stations, writers, judges, lawyers, teachers, homosexuals, Jehovah's Witnesses, and others. All these people were sent to concentration camps.

Members of the SS would play a major role in the final extermination of Jews. The men in charge of this heinous task were Adolf Eichmann and Reinhard Heydrich.

CHAPTER SEVEN

HITLER YOUTHS AND BURNING BOOKS

*T*he Nazi propaganda machine left no stone unturned. Children were organized into Hitler Youth groups. They wore swastika armbands and were taught to hate Jews. Children were taught to spy on their parents and report anyone who said anything against Hitler. A popular children's board game was called "Get the Jews Out!" By throwing dice, the winner manages to drive six Jews out of their homes and businesses. The game sold over a million copies by 1938.

The Nazis unleashed a wave of terror across Germany. Jews were attacked everywhere. Jewish shops and stores were broken into and vandalized. Himmler said that he would not use German police to protect the Jews.

Here's how the windows of a Jewish shop in Berlin looked in 1938 after being daubed with the word JUDE (Jew).

Members of a Nazi youth camp ride the backs of
their comrades. These future Nazi soldiers gallop
across a field like charioteers of old.

Although Hitler and the Nazis blamed the Jews for everything wrong with their country, Jews only made up one percent of all the people in Germany!

Jewish temples, called synagogues, were raided. Sacred Jewish objects were stomped on. Laughing, mocking men burned Jewish holy books. Goebbels fanned the flames with false stories in the press about Jews killing Aryan babies and drinking human blood. Concert halls, cafes, movie houses, and parks put up signs that read "No Jews or Dogs" or "Jews Not Allowed." In bars and cabarets Germans put on skits showing Jews as gorillas and pigs.

The attacks on the Jews got the attentions of the world. The United States began an unofficial boycott of Germany. This meant that the United States would no longer trade with Germany. It was only a partial boycott. This had little effect except stoking the Nazis' anger.

Jews throughout Germany were forced to wear a yellow Star of David sewn to their chest. This reduced them, even while free, to a slave status and free game.

In reaction to the boycott, Hitler enacted a German boycott of all Jewish business. Posters went up across Germany that read, "Germans! Defend Yourselves! Do Not Buy From Jews! Anyone Who Buys From Jews Is A Traitor!"

On April 1, 1933, the Nazi boycott began. Two black-shirted SS men stood in front of every Jewish shop. No one was allowed to enter. The word *Juden* —Jew—was painted across the store windows, or a Nazi favorite *Judah verrecke!* —Jews perish! The boycott was supposed to last five days, but it lasted only one day. Still, it struck terror into all German Jews. Acts of violence against the Jews grew in number.

On April 7, the first anti-Jewish law was passed. It was called "Law For The Restoration Of The Civil Service." It was also called the Aryan Law. All non-Aryans in the civil service were to be expelled. "Non-Aryans" were anybody who had Jewish parents or two or more Jewish grandparents.

The Aryan Laws got Jews fired from their jobs as doctors, dentists, judges, professors, and in the theater and the arts.

On May 10, thousands of university students in thirty German cities collected the works of "undesirable writers" and burned them in huge bonfires. In Berlin alone over 20,000 books were burned.

Their spirits rising with the flames, these young Nazis burst out in cheers as they salute their leader in Berlin's Opera Plaza during the book-burning orgy in which 20,000 volumes were reduced to ashes.

Goebbels made a speech at the scene. "The age of hairsplitting Jewish intellectualism is now ended," he said. "Brightened by these flames our vow shall be: The Reich and the Nation and our Führer Adolf Hitler! Heil! Heil! Heil!"

Following this example, books were removed from libraries and burned all over Germany. Soon one-third of all library books in Germany went up in flames.

Like many other Nazi propaganda efforts, the book burnings were designed to terrorize people. The massive bonfires featured torchlight parades, crazed dancing, classical music, and booming chants.

Jewish authors whose books were burned include Albert Einstein and Sigmund Freud. The books of many famous German authors, who were not Jewish, were also burned. American books by such authors as Earnest Hemingway, Jack London, Upton Sinclair, and Sinclair Lewis were burned.

Madmen had come to rule a demented society that now lived without laws. Soon they would be burning bodies instead of books.

CHAPTER EIGHT

THE LAWS OF MADNESS

As the insanity continued, Jews—who could afford to—left Germany. Most could not leave. Men who had been doctors, lawyers, and shopkeepers were taken away to slave labor camps where they were forced to move stones sixteen hours a day. Some were forced to build roads with their bare hands. Those who refused were lashed to trees and beaten.

On September 5, 1935, Hitler wrote hatred of the Jews into German law. The Nuremberg Laws were passed in two parts. One was called "The Law for the Protection of German Blood and German Honor." The second was "The Reich Citizenship Law."

Hitler displays his strength in a Nazi demonstration in 1935.

The Protection Law said that:

"Marriages between Jews and citizens of Germany or related blood are forbidden. Marriages performed despite this ban are invalid, even if performed abroad to avoid this law.

"Sexual relations between Jews and the citizens of Germany or related blood are forbidden.

"Jews may not employ in their households female citizens of Germany or related blood under 45 years old.

"Jews are not permitted to display the German flag or national colors..."

The Citizenship Law stated:

"A citizen of the Reich is only that subject of German or related blood who proves by his conduct that he is ready and able to serve the German people and the Reich faithfully.

"Only a citizen of the Reich enjoys full political rights.

"A Jew cannot be a citizen of the Reich. He has no right to vote in political affairs and he cannot hold public office."

A Jew was defined as a "person descended from at least three grandparents who are full Jews by race." Soon only one Jewish parent or grandparent was considered enough to be called a Jew.

Jews and Christians had been intermarrying for centuries. People who thought of themselves as Christian were horrified if they found that they had one Jewish grandparent. The Nazis conducted salvage hunts for these people. By law, people who were part Jewish were called *Mischlinge* —mongrels.

This sign reads "Germans don't buy in Jewish shops." Hundreds of posters asking Germans not to buy in Jewish shops were hung throughout Germany. The Nazis believed the signs would help keep customers away.

For the first time in history, Jews were persecuted because of their so-called racial identity—because of the bloodlines of their parents and grandparents.

Seven documents were needed to prove pure German heritage: a birth certificate, birth certificates for both parents, and birth certificates for all four grandparents. New industries sprang up— "licensed family researchers." These people would find the necessary documents needed to prove that a person had no Jewish blood.

Signs appeared outside cities and towns that said "JEWS NOT WANTED HERE" or "JEWS ARE OUR MISFORTUNE." Jewish people were forced out of towns where they had lived for years so that the town could declare itself *Judenrein* —cleansed of Jews.

Property owned by Jews had to be registered with the Nazis. It was then sold cheaply or given to Germans. All Jewish workers and managers were fired. German businesses got rich by taking apart Jewish firms. German banks made huge profits on the deals.

A Jewish doctor who gave his blood to save a German's life was sentenced to seventeen months in a concentration camp for "defiling the Aryan race."

The Nazis published a list of one hundred common Jewish names. If a Jewish person did not have one of those names, they had to add a so-called Jewish name to theirs. Women had to add "Sarah" men had to add "Israel" as their middle names. In this way, the Nazis could easily identify a Jewish person by his or her name.

Switzerland was afraid of being overrun by fleeing Jews. To solve this problem all passports belonging to Jews were marked with a "J" or the word *Jude*.

Seventeen thousand Polish Jews were kicked out of Germany and dumped into a small town on the Polish border. At first, the Polish government would not admit the Jews. They were forced to live for weeks in filthy stables until officials of the Polish government changed their minds.

CHAPTER NINE

CRYSTAL NIGHT

A young Jewish man in Paris was outraged by the treatment his parents were getting by the Germans. In anger, this seventeen-year-old student shot and killed a German embassy official in Paris.

The Nazis used this incident as an excuse to unleash a massive attack on Jews and their property. It became known as *Kristallnacht* or "Crystal Night—the Night of the Broken Glass" because of the huge amount of broken windows that littered the streets the next day.

On the nights of November 9 and 10, 1938, orders went out to the Gestapo to burn Jewish temples. The Nazis wanted it to look like an unofficial act carried out by angry citizens, but it was carefully planned. Notices sent to SS members in cities and towns read:

> At very short notice actions against the Jews, especially their synagogues, will take place throughout Germany.

They are not to be hindered. Such measures are to be taken that do not entail danger to German life and property. All Jewish synagogues are to be blown up or set on fire immediately. Neighboring houses occupied by Aryans are not to be damaged. This action is to be carried out in civilian clothes.

Ninety-one Jews were killed throughout the country. Over 30,000 Jewish males were sent to concentration camps. This was almost the entire male Jewish population between the ages of eighteen and sixty-five. Over 815 shops, 29 department stores, and 171 houses were destroyed. More than 190 synagogues were burned and 76 more were demolished.

A small crowd gathered outside of a Jewish shop to inspect damage done by anti-Jewish raiders.

After Crystal Night, Goering, Goebbels, and other high-ranking Nazis decided what to do next. They decreed that the Jews were to make all the needed repairs themselves and pay for them as well. All insurance money would be turned over to the Reich. Then the Jews were fined one billion reichsmarks—over $400 million. This fine was to make up for their "terrible crime" against the German people.

Jews were forced down on their hands and knees to scrub the streets clean after Crystal Night. They were guarded over by Hitler Youth and SS soldiers while crowds watched and ridiculed them.

The Nazis weren't finished. Dozens of laws were passed to destroy the Jews. All Jewish valuables had to be turned over to the Reich. Jews were not allowed to own radios, use telephones, have pets, or go to barbers or beauty salons. They could not buy food, go to school, or use swimming pools. Between 1933 and 1939, four hundred separate laws were passed to define, isolate, exclude, segregate, and impoverish German Jews.

All Jews were forced to wear the Star of David on their clothes. All Jews were eventually forced from their homes.

In September 1941, no Jews were allowed to appear in public unless they were wearing a large yellow Jewish star sewn to their clothes. For the first time since the Middle Ages, a Jewish Star of David was used as a badge of shame. In October 1941, Jews were forbidden to leave their homes. They were trapped in Germany. They could not leave.

CHAPTER TEN

NO ESCAPE FROM THE NAZIS

When Hitler came to power in 1933, there were over 500,000 Jews in Germany. By 1939, over 300,000 had left for other countries. An untold number of Jews simply committed suicide rather than live under Nazi terror. By 1941, 164,000 Jews remained in Germany, most of them in Berlin.

Leaving Germany was not easy for the Jews. They were forced to pay a heavy tax when they left and give up everything they owned. They had to start all over again with empty pockets. And this was during a worldwide economic depression. People were out of work and starving even in wealthy countries like the United States. The Jews who left Germany were forced to start all over again in a foreign country where they could not even speak the language.

In the end, it didn't matter that the Jews escaped Germany. For the Jews who fled to other European countries, the end was only delayed.

*A bus load of arrested Jews in Berlin. Scenes like this were
familiar during the first days of the Nazi boycott against the Jews.
Government officials are shown jotting down answers to their
questions before the prisoners are taken away.*

The United States had strict control over immigration and would not let most European Jews in. Many who fled Germany were simply killed later in Poland, France, the Netherlands, Hungary, or elsewhere.

The triumph of Nazism took the Jews by surprise. The laws and prejudice cut against one hundred years of tranquility in Germany. As German citizens, many Jews thought that the Nazis would soon pass. It all happened so fast, within a period of six years. The Jews saw themselves as full partners in German political, social, and cultural life.

German anti-Semitism was only a warm-up for the unspeakable horrors to come. Soon the Nazis would invade other countries in Europe and round up all the Jews they could find: Eighty-three thousand in France, over two hundred thousand each in Czechoslovakia and Hungary, one million in the Soviet Union, three million in Poland. From every corner of the continent, the Nazis searched until the number of Jews affected reached six million souls.

GLOSSARY

Annihilate - to reduce to complete ruin, to wipe out completely.

Anti-Semitism - hatred of Jews.

Assimilate - to become one with or absorb into. When the Jews became assimilated, they took up the manners and customs of another country or people.

Concentration camp - a guarded camp for the detention and forced labor of political prisoners.

Conspiracy - an evil, unlawful plot.

Descendant - one descended from another or from a common stock.

Exterminate - to destroy totally.

Genetics - the science of heredity.

Ghetto - a section of a city in most European countries where all Jews were forced to live.

Holocaust - the mass extermination of Jews in Nazi German.

Myth - a legend or story, usually one that attempts to account for something in nature.

Passover - A Jewish holiday celebrating the deliverance of the Hebrews from slavery in ancient Egypt.

Persecution - to be harassed with harsh treatment because of one's race, religion, or beliefs.

Prejudice - hatred or dislike of someone because of their race, religion, or beliefs.

Propaganda - information or ideas that are repeated over and over to change the public's thinking about an idea or group of people.

Protocol - an original draft of a document.

Racist - a person who believes that their race is superior to others.

Reichstag - the ruling body, congress, or parliament of Germany.

Repress - to keep under control or stifle another person.

Schutzstaffel (SS) - the black-shirted security squad of elite Nazis.

Semite - a member of any of a various ancient and modern people, especially Hebrews or Arabs.

Swastika - an ancient figure made of a cross with its arms bent at right angles. Native Americans take this symbol to mean good luck. The Nazis used it for their national symbol.

Synagogue - a Jewish house of worship.

BIBLIOGRAPHY

Adler, David A. *We Remember the Holocaust.* New York: Henry Holt and Company, 1989.

Aharoni, Yohanan, and Avi-Yonah, Michael. *The Macmillan Bible Atlas.* New York: Macmillan, 1993.

Ausubel, Nathan, and Gross, David C. *Pictorial History of the Jewish People.* New York: Crown Publishers, Inc., 1953, 1984.

Berenbaum, Michael. *The World Must Know.* Boston: Little, Brown and Company, 1993.

Block, Gay, and Drucker, *Malka Rescuers.* New York: Holmes & Meier Publications, Inc., 1992

Chaikin, Miriam. *A Nightmare in History: The Holocaust 1933-1945.* New York: Clarion Books, 1987.

Dawidowicz, Lucy S. *The War Against the Jews 1933-1945.* New York: Seth Press, 1986.

Flannery, Edward H. *The Anguish of the Jews.* New York: Paulist Press, 1985.

Gilbert, Martin. *Final Journey.* New York: Mayflower Books, 1979.

Gilbert, Martin. *The Macmillan Atlas of the Holocaust.* New York: Macmillan, 1982.

Greenfeld, Howard. *The Hidden Children.* New York: Ticknor & Fields, 1993.

Landau, Elaine. *The Warsaw Ghetto Uprising.* New York: New Discovery Books, 1992.

Paldiel, Mordecai. *The Path of the Righteous.* Hoboken, New Jersey: KTAV Publishing House, Inc., 1993.

Index